MEDITATION FOR BEGINNERS

Ultimate Guide To Relieve Stress, Depression And Anxiety

Sarah Rowland

Copyright © 2016 by Sarah Rowland

All rights reserved. No part of this book may be reproduced or transmitted in any form or by any means, electronic or mechanical, including photocopying, recording or by any information storage and retrieval system without written permission of the publisher, except for the inclusion of brief quotations in a review.

TABLE OF CONTENTS

INTRODUCTION 1

Chapter 1 *The Basics* 3

Chapter 2 *Practice* 34

Chapter 3 *Common Pitfalls* 47

Chapter 4 *Keys To Success* 61

Chapter 5 *Answers to Common Questions* 77

Conclusion 85

Description 86

INTRODUCTION

Congratulations on downloading this book and thank you for doing so.

The following chapters will teach you everything that you need to know about meditation so that you can easily and quickly relieve yourself of stress, anxiety, and depression.

Chapter 1 discusses the basics of meditation, such as what meditation is, the different chakras, mindfulness, as well as how to practice meditation, among others.

Chapter 2 deals with the actual practice of meditation. You will learn different kinds of meditation techniques, such as breathing meditation, mantra meditation, chakra meditation, and even a way to meet your spirit guide.

Chapter 3 talks about the common pitfalls that beginners often encounter. It is important for you to know them so that you can avoid making the same mistakes.

Chapter 4 reveals the keys to success so that you can get the best benefits from your meditation practice.

Chapter 5 gives the answers to common questions about meditation.

There are plenty of books on this subject on the market; thanks again for choosing this one! Every effort was made to ensure it is full of as much useful information as possible. Please enjoy!

CHAPTER 1
The Basics

The practice of meditation can be traced back to ancient times. It is a common practice in Buddhism, Hinduism, and in many other spiritual traditions. But, what is meditation? Some say that it is a prayer or some form of mysticism, while others say that it is an art of transforming the mind. All these definitions may be true. Meditation is not really something that you define. It is something that you practice on a regular basis, and the only way to discover its true meaning is to experience it on your own.

Today, meditation is seen as an effective way to feel better, to reduce stress and anxiety, or simply a way to get a better quality of sleep. However, it should be noted that meditation is more spiritual than physical.

Power and benefits of meditation

Meditation offers enormous benefits, from physical, mental, emotional and, of course, spiritual benefits. Today, in a world full of busy people, meditation is usually promoted as a way to relieve stress. Although relieving stress is one of the benefits of meditation, it should be noted that meditation is more spiritual than physical. It was also through years of meditation that Siddhartha Gautama Buddha achieved enlightenment.

Meditation is a powerful spiritual practice that can alter your state of mind and change your life. On a spiritual level, regular practice of meditation can make you feel calmer and improve your sleep. It can also reduce anxiety and depression. Meditation is also able to boost your immune system by suppressing the production of stress hormone. A study conducted at Harvard Medical School also revealed that regular practice of meditation can significantly lower blood pressure.

On a spiritual level, meditation is a key to enlightenment. It also strengthens the aura, energizes your chakras, and develops your psychic senses. Also, when you go deep into meditation, you can have magical and divine experiences.

How to practice meditation

The best way to practice meditation is simply to do it regularly. There are many meditation techniques that you can find online or when you read books on this subject. There is really no right or wrong way to meditate, as long as it works for you. You can try all the different meditation techniques that you can find and then stick to the one that works best.

Meditation is not something that you do sparingly. If you really want to experience the enormous benefits that it offers, then you should meditate regularly. This means that you should meditate every day, or as often as you can.

One session of meditation may last for a few minutes or up to an hour, even several hours, or even for more than a day. It is not how long you meditate that matters, but the quality of your meditation.

You should not worry about time when you meditate. When you meditate and enter deeper states of consciousness, you will lose track of time. Some moments, time may seem to fly so quickly, while other moments it might seem to move so slowly. Of course, if you are too concerned of the time, you can always set an alarm clock to signal the end of a meditation session. Just remember to use a sound that is not too high or too loud; otherwise, you might get a headache. When you go deep in meditation, even the slightest sound can be a distraction. Therefore, when you use an alarm, it is good to use a gentle or soothing music, and do not make it too loud.

Preparation

Before you start meditating, it is important for you to know the right position. There are different positions that you can use: You can meditate in a sitting or cross-legged position on the floor, or even while lying down. You can also meditate while sitting on a chair. When sitting on a chair, you should keep your spine straight and your feet flat on the floor. Having your spine straight will allow the energy in your body to flow smoothly. If sitting on a chair, having the soles of your feet flat on the floor will make you more connected to the earth and feel more grounded and centered.

If you sit on the floor to meditate, you can put a cushion or a towel under your legs or knees to help you feel more comfortable. Again, the important part is to keep your spine straight.

Whether or not you should close your eyes while meditating is a matter of personal preference. But, to minimize distraction and feel more relaxed, it is recommended that you close your eyes when meditating.

You should, of course, choose a time that you will not be distracted. Turn your phone off or switch it to silent mode prior to meditation. Also, avoid wearing tight clothing, so that you will not feel uncomfortable. To be more comfortable, it is also suggested that you remove your shoes.

Many of those who meditate regularly like to create a special place where they do their meditation practice. It does not have to be a big space. In fact, it can be as simple as having a meditation space in a small corner of your room. After all, you do not move to places when you meditate, except when you practice walking meditation.

The moment of *Now*

All meditation techniques teach that you should exist and be present in the *Now*. Unfortunately, many people these days are unconscious of what they are doing. Meditation teaches that you should be here now, live, and experience life as it is. It should be noted that experiencing being present in the moment of *Now* is not a strange idea. One way or another, you have experienced this already. This is the moment when it seems like everything has fallen into place, or during moments of extreme emotions. For example, in a game of basketball, this is the time when a player is said to be "on fire." This moment can also be how you felt when you had your first intimate kiss with your loved one, where every small movement or sound felt so meaningful.

Imagination

Imagination is a key to enter a higher state of consciousness. It will allow you to visit a realm that would otherwise be hidden from the reality that you usually know. Some meditation techniques, especially those that deal with pathworking, will ask you to imagine a scene. For example, imagine walking on the shore. When you do this, it is important that you keep an open mind. Allow the imagined scene to unfold. Now, you might be wondering, "Is it real?" The answer to this question is still under controversy. Some believe that since you only deal with imagined scenes or objects, then it could not be real. However, there are those who believe that even imagined things somehow have an existence of their own. After all, simply having something in your mind already proves the fact that it exists. Otherwise, it could not even exist in your mind. Regardless whether you want to believe them to be real or not, the effects that they do remain beneficial. So, just try the meditation techniques in this book, and see for yourself.

A committee of minds

When you meditate, you may notice that you seem to have different minds. This is due to the fact that you have diverse ideas, and there are different ways to satisfy each one of them. Such ideas may vary from your different notions of what happiness is, how to satisfy different kinds of pleasure, up to your definition of yourself. By practicing meditation, you can get to still your minds and make them be in harmony with one another.

On mindfulness

Meditation teaches one to be mindful. This means that you should be conscious and truly exist in the present moment. Unfortunately, many people are not conscious of being alive. Such "unconsciousness" explains why even after talking to someone, you cannot even tell what the person is wearing, or not noticing the color of the ceiling even when you have been in the room for more than an hour already. Many people get used to their daily routine that they become like robots. Meditation seeks to remedy this problem by teaching you to be conscious and experience the beauty of being truly alive, where every breath matters.

How to use meditation to find true happiness from within

Any meditation technique can lead you to find inner happiness. When you meditate, you get to be in touch with the divine energy, and you get to discover your own divinity. This is not hard to achieve. In fact, in the first few days that you begin meditating, you may already feel some sort of happiness that explodes from within. As you continue to meditate, this happiness grows, and you will be able to tap it even when not meditating. It simply becomes a part of you. The key to finding true happiness from within is simply to meditate regularly.

It is important to note that true happiness does not just come by meditating. To make happiness real, there must also be a change of heart. When you meditate for a longer time, you may notice that you become kinder and gentler, especially if you regularly work on your heart chakra. You should allow such positive changes to manifest themselves through your actions. You also cannot expect to have a peaceful and happy life if you are not at peace with yourself. By meditating, you get to still the mind and free your real self. Making peace with yourself is often the key to improving your relationship with other people. Simply put, the practice of meditation will give you a sense of peace and happiness, but if you want to make such development to be meaningful, then you should share such positive energies with everyone.

What is a mantra?

A mantra is a word, syllable, or sound, that functions as the point of focus in meditation. The most common mantra is the mantra *OM* or *AUM*. This mantra is usually practiced in Buddhism, Hinduism, as well as in other spiritual traditions. According to Pranic Healing Grandmaster Choa Kok Sui, the mantra *OM* was the very first sound in the universe.

There are different kinds of mantras. In fact, you can even make your own mantra. By having a mantra to focus on, you get to shut other thoughts from entering your mind. And, in case other thoughts are able to penetrate your mind, you can avoid clinging to these thoughts simply by shifting your focus back on your mantra. Again, your mantra is your point of focus in meditation. Remember: When you meditate, nothing should exist in your mind, except your mantra.

Meditation is a holy pilgrimage, and your mantra is the vehicle that you use to reach your destination. Therefore, it is important that you learn to be one with your mantra. Of course, the way to do this is to keep on chanting your mantra and meditating regularly.

Monkey mind

When you first start meditating, you may find that it is hard to control your thoughts. Many thoughts may arise as you meditate, such as what are you going to have for dinner, things that you need to do for work or school, some people that you need to talk to, or even if what you are doing actually makes any sense. In Buddhism, this is called as the *monkey mind*, where your mind jumps from one thought to another, just like a monkey jumping from one branch to another. Do not worry; this is normal. With consistent practice, you will be able to overcome this monkey mind. Remember that during meditation, you should be in the present moment called *Now*. Do not entertain other thoughts. After all, you can deal with your other concerns *after* meditation.

The chakras

The term *chakra* is a Sanskrit word which means *wheel*. The chakras are the energy centers in the body. The body, more specifically, your energy body, has seven major chakras located along the spine. On the one hand, when any of these chakras is not properly balanced, you may experience discomfort, serious stress, or even illness. On the other hand, if you have well-energized chakras, then you can enjoy a healthy body and a positive living. Having healthy chakras is also the way to a healthy body. It should be noted, however, that the physical body and the energy body are closely connected. If you want to have healthy chakras, you also need to take care of your physical body.

Crown chakra

The crown chakra is located just a little above your head. This chakra serves as the entry point for higher consciousness. This is the key to connecting with the higher self and cosmic consciousness. This chakra is strongly associated with divine intelligence and wisdom. Those with high spiritual realization have a more developed crown chakra. This is also what is symbolized by the crowns worn by kings and other royalties. The crown chakra is important in realizing the oneness of spirituality. It also affects your state of mind and how you think. When you develop your crown chakra, you should also work on your heart chakra. The color of this chakra is violet.

Ajna chakra

The ajna chakra, or more popularly known as the *third eye chakra*, is the seat of the intuition, which allows you to see psychic and spiritual visions. It is located between the eyebrows. If you want to develop psychic abilities such as clairvoyance, telepathy, remote viewing, and channeling, then this is the chakra that you should work on. The ajna chakra will allow you to see things as they truly are. When you first start to develop this chakra, the visions that you will get may not be as clear and correct as they should be. However, the visions will gradually improve, and you will get vivid and solid visions, and even see spirits in the astral dimension or the Otherworld. The color of this chakra is indigo.

Throat chakra

If you are having trouble with expressing yourself, then you should work on your throat chakra. Located in the throat, it is the realm of creative expression. It is about communication and voicing the truth. It should be noted that this chakra is not just about talking, but it also emphasizes the importance of listening.

After all, every good communicator knows that listening is more important than talking. The color of this chakra is blue.

Heart chakra

The heart chakra is the center of universal love. It is located in the center of the chest at the level of the physical heart. If you are wondering why all the enlightened beings who walked the earth were so kind and loving, then the heart chakra explains it all. Although this chakra may be associated with romantic love shared between two people, the chakra is more about the universal type of love, such as love for your enemies, neighbors, and even for strangers. This chakra is an important part of any spiritual transformation. If you want to be more forgiving and kind, then you should work on your heart chakra. The color of this chakra is green.

Solar plexus chakra

The solar plexus chakra is associated with willpower. It is located in the solar plexus region. Since the meaningful things in life always require the exercise of willpower, this chakra is something that you cannot ignore. When you feel powerless and controlled by other people instead of being the master of your life, then it is usually a sign that you need to strengthen your solar plexus chakra. A common cause of an underdeveloped solar plexus chakra is when a child receives lots of discouragements instead of inspirations and motivations. The color of this chakra is yellow.

Sacral chakra

The sacral chakra, also known as *sex chakra* or *belly chakra,* is located about two inches below the navel. This chakra deals with sexuality and does not just refer to the mere act of lovemaking. It is also associated with expression through the sense of touch, such as an embrace. After all, procreation is only possible when there is an expression of strong emotions. If you have problems with your sexual life or in controlling your lust, or if you simply want to last longer in bed, then this chakra is something that you cannot ignore. The color of this chakra is orange.

Root chakra

This chakra is also known as the *base chakra.* It is located at the base of the spine and deals with security and safety. Located beneath the other main chakras, it also serves as a foundation. A strong base chakra will make you feel more grounded and stable. This chakra deals with the basic needs, such as a food and shelter.

It also refers to your emotional and even spiritual needs. It is also the point for kundalini awakening. The color of this chakra is red.

Chakra colors

Knowing the colors of each chakra is essential so that you will know the right way to visualize the chakras during meditation. Although most meditation techniques do not require that you visualize any of the chakras, there are some techniques that will require you to *see* the chakras. By knowing their respective colors, you will be more able to connect with them.

Memorizing the colors of the seven chakras is very simple. As you may notice, they follow the colors of the rainbow: ROYGBIV. Where *R* or *Red* is the root chakra, and then up to *V* or *Violet* for the crown chakra.

What is the mind?

When you read about meditation, books on the subject always mention the word *mind*. But, what is this mind? Does it refer to your brain? It should be noted that mind in meditation does not only refer to your brain or your thoughts, but covers a more comprehensive meaning. In fact, it does not even refer to your mind. The mind is something that you do not see with your eyes.

But, if the mind is not the brain or any other physical part that you can see, what can it be?

It should be understood that the mind and the body are two different things. For example, you can be very inactive in bed, but have wild and wonderful thoughts in your mind. The mind is formless. Some people figuratively call it the "heart." Like, when someone loves a person, he says that the person he loves is in his heart, yet he obviously does not refer to his physical heart. Now, it is important to control the mind, because happiness depends heavily on one's state of mind.

Levels of consciousness

When you meditate, you enter into different states of consciousness. The levels that you experience depend on how deep you are in meditation. There are seven states of consciousness, and they are the following:

The first three states are your normal waking consciousness, when you are in a deep sleep, and the state of dreaming. These three states are very much known to man, even to those who do not practice meditation. There are, however, three more states of consciousness that are rarely experienced.

The fourth state of consciousness is known as the transcendental consciousness. This is the state of total silence where the mind and all your senses are still; however, unlike sleeping, your consciousness remains awake so you are able to tell what is happening. Some meditators confuse this state with the devil's realm because you will experience a sense of bliss in this state. However, it should be noted that once you enter this state, you must keep on continuing your meditation, because there are other states to reach, and this should not be the end goal of meditation. But, if you only want to experience bliss and feel calmer, then this state of consciousness will not disappoint you.

The fifth level of consciousness is called cosmic consciousness. Here, you realize total detachment from the self and realize that you are nothing but consciousness. In this state, you will understand that you are not the body or the mind. You are only a consciousness. It is in this state where the ego totally disappears. And, by discovering what you are not, you get to realize who you truly are. This state of consciousness can be likened to the parable of the white room. The parable goes something like this: A man is in a white room all his life. One day, a ball enters the room, and he realizes that he is not the ball. The next day, an elephant enters, and he realizes that he is also not an elephant. The following day, an airplane enters the room, and he realizes that he is not an airplane, and so on and so forth. The more things that enter the room, the more he realizes who he is not; and by knowing who he is not, he gets to realize who he truly is. When you reach the fifth level of consciousness, the ego dissolves, the body and your sense of self get detached, and you realize that you are nothing but consciousness.

Again, this stage is not the end. Although what you can experience here would be mystifying, you must continue to meditate. If you use mantra meditation, then keep focusing on your mantra, for this is not the end of your spiritual pilgrimage.

The sixth level of consciousness is called God consciousness. Again, many meditators confuse this with the devil's realm. But, take note that this is not the final stage of meditation. When you reach this state, you will experience a feeling of great bliss. This is the state where you totally lose the self and find the Self, which is the divinity that lies within. It is during this state where you will feel your heart open up and experience a state of bliss that appears to be the purest of anything. If you are familiar with the Christian text that says that humans are made in the image and likeness of God, then this state of consciousness will make you feel, realize, and experience its true meaning. For, after all, there is divinity within each person. In this stage, you shall get in touch and experience that divinity, which is part of the divine essence of things.

The seventh level of consciousness, which is the highest state, is the unity consciousness. This is the stage of enlightenment and is the last stage of meditation. It may take you years to reach this stage. In Buddhism, this is the state of Nirvana, or eternal happiness. Here there is no more division between the inner and the outer, between the self and the Self, but everything reveals itself as one. This is the true realization of the oneness of spirituality. In this state, you experience and realize that the self and the Divine are one and the same, that you have always been part of the Divine energy. Indeed, here you will know that you are not simply made in the image and likeness of God, but that you have a god-self, where the divinity that lies within reveals itself completely.

Effects of stress, anxiety, and depression

The effects of stress, anxiety, depression, and all other negativity are harmful to your health and wellbeing. When you are in a state of negativity, the chakras weaken and blockages are made which prevent the smooth flow of energy. If left untreated, illness, disease, and other serious side effects can be expected to manifest in the physical body.

By practicing meditation, you can avoid the aforesaid side effects. It also does not matter which meditation technique you use, since all forms of meditation strengthen the aura, as well as your chakras and energy body.

You should understand that negative energies such as anxiety and stress are not good and that you always have a choice whether you want your life to be controlled by these negative forces or not. Let me repeat: You have a choice. If feeling stressed is something that you cannot control, just remember a saying in Buddhism: "If you can solve your problems, what is the use of worrying? If you cannot solve your problems, what is the use of worrying?" Therefore, do not worry. Worrying will only make you feel stressed out and create blockages.

Regardless what negative energy you are dealing with, meditation can help you feel so much better. But, just like any medicine, it may take time for you to actually feel the benefits of meditation. But, take note that no amount of meditation is ever wasted. You should meditate and persevere. If you do so, your perspective and mindset will change, and you can exercise mastery not just over you healthy, but also over yourself.

On happiness

Happiness is possible and is always within your reach regardless of your circumstances in life. Being happy is a state of mind, and it is a choice — a choice that only you can make. The good news is that meditation is a key to happiness. If you persist in this practice, you will soon discover a happiness that is impossible to describe, and this happiness can be eternal. Once you go deep in meditation and discover the mystery of a single breath or the beauty if a mantra, you will know that happiness has always been with you and that you only need to look within to find it.

Increase your vibration

Meditation is an effective way to increase your vibration. Your vibration is what controls your mental state. You draw certain energies or influences depending on your level of vibration. Negative and filthy things are associated with low vibrations, while pleasant things are associated with high vibrations. Now, you might be wondering, "How do I increase my vibration?" According to the Hermetic teachings, the way to increase your vibration can be done by using your will. You should use your will to focus on something that is positive and ignore negativity. Just simply focus and work on positive things. Take note that you do not deal directly with the negative stuff. This is because of the esoteric teaching that positive and negative are one and the same. They are only different in terms of degree. Also, even assuming that you removing a negative trait or quality, what then goes in its place? If nothing, then you will be left with emptiness even after removing a particular negativity. But, by working on positive energies, the negative qualities do not just disappear, but you also fill your life with happy, peaceful, and pleasant energies.

Remaining in a state of good vibration may be challenging. There are many things in life that can affect your mood and suddenly change your vibration. However, with persistence and continuous practice, you can maintain a state of high vibration for a longer period of time. Mastery of the self is the key.

What is the energy body?

As you read this book or any book in meditation, you will usually encounter the term *energy body*. Now, what is the energy body? Obviously, it does not refer to your physical body. Unless, if you want to consider your physical your body as a form of energy, which it is, then you may understand the term energy body to also refer to your physical body — which is fine. But, usually, the term energy body refers to that body that you have that is usually invisible to the naked eye. Taking care of your energy body is important because it strongly affects your physical body. In fact, a study shows that illnesses first manifest themselves in the energy body before they manifest in the physical body. This means that a healthy energy body translates to a healthy physical body. The good news is that the regular practices of meditation naturally strengthen your energy body. It is also worth noting that the energy body can be further classified into five layers:

The etheric body is that energy body that is just less than an inch away from your physical body. This is also the energy body that can easily be seen even by the naked eye under right circumstances. It is usually referred to as a blueprint of the physical body. After the etheric energy body, the next layer is called the emotional body or emotional energy body. As the name implies, this energy body acts as the storage of different emotions and feelings, such as your greatest joys and fears. This energy body usually changes depending on your current emotion or state of mind.

Right after the emotional body, there is the mental energy body. This energy body is composed of your so many ideas. Your thoughts arise and are stored in this energy body. This is also the reason why you should always think of happy and positive thoughts. If you keep on thinking negative thoughts, your mental energy body can be easily contaminated. Last but not least is the spiritual energy body. This energy body is usually associated with higher awareness.

It is worth noting that the different energy bodies, including your physical body, are interconnected. Each energy body can greatly affect the others. For example, when you always think positive thoughts, your mental energy body gets filled with positive energy, and since thoughts affect your emotions, even your emotional energy body gets affected. If any of your energy bodies carry positive energy, then it also reflects on your physical body. For example, by having an emotional energy body that is full of happy energy, your physical body also tends to reflect it by smiling or laughing. On a negative note, however, when your energy body is full of negativity, your physical body will also suffer. Therefore, it is important that you maintain a positive outlook and state of mind. The key to doing this is to learn to control your thoughts, and the best way to have mastery over your thoughts is by regular practice of meditation.

Signs of progress

Continuous practice is the key to progress in meditation. However, when you meditate on your row, it may be hard for you to measure or tell if you are getting any progress or not. Unfortunately, many people stop meditating because they think that they do not get any progress. It should be noted that no meditation practice is ever wasted, so do not think that you are not making any progress even if you do not notice any changes. Here are some signs that usually mean that you are progressing in your meditation practice:

More concentration – You may notice that your concentration has strengthened. This is a normal effect of any meditation technique. You will know that you develop more concentration when you can focus on your mantra (or any point of focus in meditation) without being distracted for a longer period.

Mystical experiences – Mystical experiences while meditating is also a common sign of progress. Do you see magical visions or feel an indescribable sense of bliss? This may also include simpler occurrences, such as having a rhythmic breathing, losing track of time, or seeing lights.

Posture is easily maintained – Pain or discomfort is common, especially when one has just started practicing meditation. However, as you progress in your meditation by your continuous practice, you may notice that your posture problems or discomfort suddenly disappear. Some people slouch when they meditate and feel uneasiness in their back to maintain the right posture. If you are one of these people but then suddenly notice that you have become used to the proper posture, then congratulate yourself for a nice progress.

Being more conscious during the waking state – Progress in meditation can also be seen not just during actual meditation, but also after meditation. Are you more conscious of yourself and the world during your normal state of consciousness? Those who progress in meditation tend to get more sensitive and become more appreciative of everything. In fact, even a flower or a sunset can become more beautiful than it used to be.

Time passes

As you go deeper into meditation, the more it would seem that time passes more quickly. If you find it easy to meditate for an hour without falling asleep, then it is a good sign that you are getting some progress.

Kindness

Since meditation develops the heart chakra, meditators also tend to be kind. If you notice yourself being kinder or nicer to everyone, then it may be another good sign of progress. After all, the true effects of meditation should be seen even when not meditating. Meditation should improve your character.

What other people say

Sometimes, it is what other people say that can make you realize any progress. It is not uncommon to be disappointed with a few failures that you miss out the good ones.

CHAPTER 2
Practice

Now that you have a basic knowledge of meditation, it is time for you to learn what meditation really is, and the only way to do this is by actual experience. The following will teach you various meditation techniques. Feel free to try each one of them. If getting enlightened is your goal, then it is suggested that you focus on mantra or breathing meditation. When you do any of these exercises, be sure to do so in a place where you will not be distracted. You also have to assume a proper asana or posture. As already mentioned in the previous chapter, you may meditate in a sitting position, or even while lying in bed. Should you choose to assume a lying down position, just remember that it may increase the chances of falling asleep. Regardless which position you use, the important thing is to keep your spine straight, so that the divine energy can flow smoothly and naturally.

You should also connect your tongue to your palate or the roof of your mouth. Such position improves the flow of energy and instantly strengthens the aura. You might find this uncomfortable in the beginning, but simply give yourself time to get used to it. In fact, as you get deeper in meditation, the tongue automatically connects itself to the palate.

Breathing meditation *(Duration: at least 5 minutes)*

Meditation on the breath is the simplest form of meditation. After all, what could be simpler than breathing? Although very simple, it is very effective. In fact, many meditators spend years by only practicing breathing meditation. This meditation technique has all the benefits that you can expect from meditation, such as relaxation, mental alertness, better quality of sleep, inner sense of peace and happiness, as well as spiritual awakening, among others.

1. Assume a proper position for meditation.
2. Close your eyes and relax.
3. Focus on your breathing. Your breathing is your mantra.
4. Should other thoughts arise, stay calm and relaxed, and gently focus back on your breathing.
5. Breathe in, and out.
6. Relax.

(Wait for at least five minutes)

7. Gently, bring your attention back to your physical body.
8. It is time to return to normal consciousness.
9. Slowly, open your eyes.

Mantra meditation *(Duration: at least 5 minutes)*

Mantra meditation is as common as breathing meditation, and it is very effective. Of course, the first step is for you to have a mantra. A recommended mantra to use is the mantra *OM*. When you say your mantra, you should pronounce it with a resonating sound.

If you want, you can also make your own mantra. Your mantra can be anything. It can be a word or even just a syllable. If you choose to use your own mantra, just remember that your mantra should not evoke images or emotions in your mind. Therefore, do not use the mantra *car* because it will compel you to imagine a car. Also, avoid using long mantras, so you will not have any problem with memorizing and pronouncing it over and over again.

1. Close your eyes.

2. Relax.

3. Chant your mantra.

4. Focus on your mantra.

5. Nothing should exist but your mantra.

6. Focus and be one with your mantra.

7. Let go of everything. Embrace your mantra.

8. Once you want to end the meditation session, just gently think of your body, and then slowly open your eyes.

Chakra meditation *(Duration: at least 25 minutes)*

This meditation will energize your chakras, cleanse negative energies, and remove any blockages. The steps are as follows:

Close your eyes. Relax. Inhale. As you exhale, imagine exhaling all the stress and tensions in your body. Take a slow, deep breath. Exhale. Imagine white light descending from heaven. It is a divine light, powerful, pure white, and radiant. See and feel it descend down to your crown chakra, charging it with energy.

See your crown chakra and its violet color radiating stronger, and stronger. Keep charging your crown chakra. Remember that this ray of energy is pure, powerful, and infinite. See your crown chakra glowing, getting more powerful every second.

Now, let the ray of divine light descend more, and feel as it enters the top of your head. Feel its purity and invigorating energy. See and feel as it touches your third eye chakra. Your third eye chakra is the seat of intuition. See its indigo color shining brightly as it is being charged with the divine ray of energy. As your third eye chakra gets stronger and stronger, you know that you can see through everything. Nothing can be hidden from you, because your intuition and psychic vision can penetrate through everything. Keep on charging your third eye. Feel the immense power that you are receiving.

Slowly, the divine light descends down to the next chakra, your throat chakra. Let is energize your throat chakra. Imagine yourself being comfortable in a conversation, expressing your wonderful thoughts. See yourself and everyone else smiling. You are a good communicator. You have raw creative talents. Keep charging your throat chakra. Know that the more you charge it, the better you become.

See the white light flow down slowly into your heart chakra. Imagine yourself with your family and friends having a good time. Imagine soldiers shaking hands and embracing one another. See yourself doing good deeds to people. How does it feel to love and be loved, all the time? See and feel your heart chakra expanding and glowing, so bright it is blinding. After all the hate, now you realize that you carry universal love inside you. Keep charging your heart chakra. Feel the love and all the positive energies in the universe. All these, are now in your heart.

Relax. Now exercise some love, let go of the ray of light, and let it descend down to your solar plexus chakra. This is the center of your will. The more you charge this chakra, the stronger your willpower becomes. Like a sponge, absorb the energy from the ray of white light. See your solar plexus chakra get stronger. It is glowing. The more you feed it with energy, the more it glows. Keep charging it, so that you can have a will of steel. You are strong.

Gently, direct the light to flow down to your sacral chakra. This is your sex chakra, the realm of sexuality. See the ray of light charging your sex chakra. Do you see how much the orange color of your sex chakra is growing? Imagine being engaged in a hot, steamy, lovemaking session. Feel the arousal and the passion. Do you like it? Shift your focus back to the ray of light. See and feel how it charges your sex chakra.

Finally, let the ray of light descend down to your root chakra. Remember that this chakra's color is red, and it signifies security and safety. The more you charge this aura, the more grounded and secure you will become. Feel how the ray of divine light charges your root chakra. Nothing is impossible for this divine light. The more it charges you, the more centered and grounded you become. You are one with Mother Earth. Keep charging. See the red color glowing brightly. It is blinding. You are safe.

Slowly, see and feel the divine ray of light return back to heaven. From your root chakra, feel it move up slowly to your energized sacral chakra, then slowly up your powerful solar plexus chakra, gently up to your loving heart chakra, and slowly to your throat *chakra. Gently, see the ray of light withdraw upwards to your all-seeing third eye chakra, and then as it leaves through your crown chakra, smile and thank the divine ray of light from heaven. Watch it move up to heaven and slowly disappear.*

Keep your eyes closed. See and feel the seven main chakras of your body glowing brightly. You are strong, powerful, and healthy. You are divine. Place your hands on your chest, inhale slowly — and as you inhale, imagine inhaling the energy of love and kindness. Exhale gently. Say your thanks to the universe, and slowly open your eyes.

Inner light meditation *(Duration: at least 10 minutes)*

This is another interesting meditation technique, where you only need to focus on the *light*. Try not to fall asleep. The steps are as follows:

1. Close your eyes.

2. Relax.

3. Gently focus on the *light*. Everything that you see that is not *black* is considered light.

4. If visions appear, then shift your attention and focus on the visions.

5. Simply relax and let go.

(Give this meditation technique at least 10 minutes.)

6. Gently, think of your physical body. Slowly move your toes, and then your fingers. Slowly, open your eyes.

Spirit guide meditation *(Duration: at least 30 minutes)*

It is believed that every person has a spirit guide. A spirit guide is someone who looks after your spiritual development and guides you in your spiritual journey. Some people call it a guardian angel. This meditation will allow you to meet your spirit guide and bond with him or her. The steps are as follows:

Imagine yourself standing in front of your physical body. See your physical body still and meditating. Look at your face, your shoulders, and your feet. You look safe, beautiful, and relaxed. Now, look at the room and all the things around you. You are outside your body, yet you and the universe continue to exist.

Slowly walk to your door. Open it. When opening the door, you see a vast forest in front of you. See the trees and the grass just outside your door. Know that if you step on the grass, you will be transported into another dimension — a realm where everything is possible. Your spirit guide is waiting for you in the forest. If you sincerely want to meet your spirit guide, then take a step.

Feel the grass below your feet. Feel the air blowing, and hear the leaves shaken by the wind. Walk into the forest. Maintain a straight path, so that you can easily find your way back later. What do you see? Are there animals around? Continue to walk into the forest. Do you hear the birds chirping?

As you journey deep into the forest, you see a large clearing in front of you. In the center of the clearing stands your spirit guide smiling at you. What does your spirit guide look like? Is your guide a male or a female? Is it even human? A spirit guide can be any form: human, animal, plant, or even just a ball of energy. Just be open to anything and see.

Approach your guide and greet him. Now, feel free to talk with your guide about anything. If you want, you can take a walk in the forest or just stay in the clearing and enjoy your moment together. Most of the time, guides communicate telepathically, so you might get impressions, thoughts, and images, from your guide. Take a moment now with your guide.

The sun begins to set and your guide escorts you back to the door that leads to your room. Thank your guide and enter your room.

Watch your body in the room. It is time to get back into your body. Simply will yourself back and enter your body. Now, slowly move your toes, then your fingers. And gently, open your eyes.

Healing meditation *(Duration: at least 15 minutes)*

Take as much time as you can when you do this meditation. It is important to not just visualize the light, but you should also feel its healing quality. Of course, faith is also important.

Assume a meditative position. Make sure that your spine is straight and that you are relaxed. Imagine a brilliant ray of white light descends from the heavens. It is a divine healing light. Anything and everything that it touches gets healed and rejuvenated. Now, see and feel it enter the top of your head.

Slowly, it fills your entire head. Feel the strong, powerful healing energy. Let it descend down your throat, and then down your chest and shoulders. Let the intense healing light fill every space. Feel and absorb the healing energy. Now, let the light descend down your arms, to your hands. Let it flow down your stomach, then gently down your legs, until your whole body is covered with intense, white healing light. Keep charging yourself with this healing energy. The more you charge yourself, the stronger you glow.

Once you are ready to end the meditation, simply imagine the ray of light slowly disappears. Thank the universe, and then gently open your eyes. You are healed.

Walking meditation

Although meditation is usually practiced while sitting or lying down, some meditation techniques are done in a standing position, or even while walking. A good example of this is the walking meditation. It is good to do this meditation when you go out for a stroll. The steps are simple: Simply walk around but be conscious every movement. You may want to start slow, and then gradually increase the pace as you get used to it. Surprising as it may be, you might just appreciate how wonderful the simple act of walking can be. Just like other meditations, you should be able to clear your mind and simply focus on your walk. Take note that you should focus on the act of moving and not on the surrounding scene. Therefore, feel how your feet touch and leave the floor, as well as how you breathe as you move. Feel every movement and just relax. If your thoughts start to wonder, just stop and relax for a while, and then simply start over again. If you want some light exercise, then going for a walking meditation can be your best choice. In fact, you can also do this when you go to the mall to buy something.

CHAPTER 3
Common Pitfalls

Here are the common pitfalls that beginners make when they meditate. It is best that you pay careful attention to each of them so that you will not commit the same mistakes.

Expectations

Having expectations can ruin a meditation. When you meditate, you should not expect anything to happen; otherwise, your focus and energy will be divided. For example, when you do a breathing meditation, simply focus on your breathing, and do not think of getting any sense of peace or calmness. Allow things to unfold as they are without you controlling them. A common pitfall with regard to having expectations is forcing yourself not to expect. When this happens, your focus divided. The solution here is simply not to care about what will happen. Simply do the steps of the meditation technique that you are using without any regard as to what may happen.

Analyzing

This is a common mistake committed by almost all beginners. It is important that you do not analyze anything when you meditate. This is also the reason why it is important to know the steps even before you engage in the actual practice of meditation. When you meditate, everything should flow naturally. Never analyze whether what you are doing is correct or not. Otherwise, you will end up analyzing and not meditating. Some meditators advice that you should not research so much about the meditation technique that you want to use, because sometimes having too much knowledge can be a disadvantage, especially if you still have not achieved a good level of spirituality.

Wrong posture

Maintaining a proper form or posture is important in meditation. Whether you meditate while sitting or lying down, the important thing is to keep your spine straight. This is to ensure a steady and smoother flow of energy in the body.

No slouching. Make sure that your seven main chakras are aligned. It is worth noting that there are some meditation techniques that can be done even without assuming the recommended posture. However, such kind of meditation techniques is rare.

Meditating when sleepy

It is not recommended to meditate when you are sleepy. This is because you can easily fall asleep. When you are sleepy, it is a sign that your body needs to rest, and there is no better rest than having a good sleep. If you always feel sleepy when meditating, try to meditate in the morning just a few minutes after you wake up. Although you can also meditate at night before bed, it is not good when you are too tired. Do not worry; just continuously meditate and you will get better at it.

Another reason why meditating in bed may not always be a good choice is because the bed signals sleep to your body. That is why many meditators pick to not use their bed when they meditate. But, this is a matter of personal preference. There are also those who meditate while sitting or lying in their bed and get good results.

Meditating right after eating

It is not recommended to meditate right after eating. This is because the body functions and uses energy to digest the food. When you meditate, every part of your body should be still and relaxed, and all your energy must be devoted to meditation. The energy body has many spiritual nerves, and these nerves get heavy after eating a big meal, which will prevent you from reaching a high state of consciousness. When you meditate at the right time, you will usually feel your body get lighter and lighter; however, when you meditate after a big meal, your energy body also tend to get "heavy," and it will be hard for you to reach a higher state of mind. So, it is recommended that you meditate on an empty stomach. Mornings are excellent for this. But, you can also meditate after about two hours from your last meal. If hunger bothers you when meditating, you can try to eat or drink something light, such as a glass of milk, a small cookie, or a glass of juice.

Focus on *focusing*

This is a common problem usually faced by beginners. Take note that there is a difference between focusing on your mantra and focusing on focusing on your mantra. When you focus on your mantra, you do not even think about focusing. Instead, your mind gets filled with the mantra.

To focus means to bring your attention to something, and you can do this with the mere exercise of the will. It is worth noting that when meditating, your focus should be relaxed, without any pressure or tension. How long you can remain focused also matter. Some people

Ego

To progress in meditation, there must be a destruction of the ego. It is important that you forget who you are or what you are good at, and *just be*. Ego is one of the things that hinder spiritual development. Learn to drop your ego and submit your whole self to your mantra.

A good way to deal with the ego is simply to drop it and not give it any attention. Also, stay humble even when you notice some developments. Know that there is still a long way ahead of you. Meditation is also not a competition on which one is holier. You do not have to compare yourself with others. Meditation is a personal journey — a spiritual pilgrimage.

Ego is not just an obstacle during meditation. It is also a hindrance to spiritual development. It is worth noting, however, that dropping your ego is not the same as lack of confidence. Having confidence is good, but too much of it is not.

Never compare yourself with others, especially when you experience spiritual developments. If you do compare, then compare your progress with those who have a higher state of spirituality than you. Ego is a tricky thing. Stay humble; stay true; stay pure.

Fasting

Fasting is not always a bad thing. In fact, it is also healthy. However, fasting can make it harder for you to focus. It is simply hard to focus on something when you are feeling very hungry. For beginners, fasting is not advisable. You must try to be as relaxed and comfortable as you can. Take note that fasting is not necessary.

Focusing on the visions

When you meditate, visions will start to appear. When this happens, simply focus on your mantra, except if the meditation technique that you use is really meant trigger some visions. Although it is easy to get tempted to focus on the visions instead since they may seem to be magical, such is not a good practice because it will not advance your spiritual development.

Some people may confuse these visions with lucid dreaming, or the ability to be conscious in one's dreams. Although this is possible when one meditates, there are different other visions and experiences that you may encounter. Again, just remember to focus on your mantra or the main point of the meditation technique that you are using.

Depending on meditation

It is wrong to depend too much on meditation. Some people use meditation as an excuse for mere laziness or irresponsibility. Some things in life cannot be solved just by meditating. For example, if you have financial problems, meditating even the whole day and night will not earn you any money. Remember that meditation is a spiritual pilgrimage and not a way to be lazy and irresponsible. Some people think that they progress spiritually by simply doing meditation and nothing else. Just think about it: What use is spirituality if you have no time to love or be loved by someone? What use is being compassionate if you distance yourself from people who need compassion?

Doubts

Doubts in the meditation technique that you are using, especially doubt in yourself, can ruin your meditation. Have faith and never doubt. If you should doubt a particular technique or anything else, entertain your doubts after meditation. But, during meditation, you must let go of doubts and simply be present in the moment of Now.

Once you entertain doubts, you will get divided and it will be impossible to achieve a higher state if consciousness. Also, doubting shifts your mindset into an analytical state of mind, which is not good for any form of meditation. When you meditate, you should let go of everything, especially your doubts.

Worrying

Some beginners usually worry while meditating. They feel itchy and their legs feel numb after some minutes of being engaged in meditation. It should be noted that the practice of meditation is safe. When you feel your legs get numbed, which usually happens when you meditate in a cross-legged position, it is nothing to worry about because it is normal. In fact, the deeper you go into meditation, the more you will not feel your physical body — where literally nothing will exist but your mantra. Needless to say, feeling some parts of your body getting itchy is also normal and is something that you should not allow yourself to get distracted with.

Don't worry be happy

Of course, worry may come in the form of your real-life problems, for example, money problems or relationship problems. Although you should deal with such problems, you should understand that the time for doing meditation is not the time to think of such problems. Do not worry; you have all the time to think of those problems *after* meditation. But, during meditation, only focus on your mantra and still your mind.

Negative thoughts

Avoid negative thoughts. In fact, never entertain any negative thought. This is true whether you are engaged in actual meditation or not. Of course, this does not mean that you will be blind to any form of negativity. Rather, this simply means that you notice any negative thoughts but do not cling to any of them. According to ancient teachings in alchemy, the proper way to deal with negative thoughts is not to deal with them directly. Instead, you should just focus on the opposite, which is the positive side. For example, if you have thoughts that make you sad, then think and do things that will make you happy. By doing so, the negative energy will disappear on its own.

Another effective way to deal with negativity is to use affirmations. For example, if you think that you cannot do any meditation properly because you do not feel at peace due to lots of random thoughts, you can use an affirmation that will give you the right and positive mindset. For example, you can use the affirmation, "I am at peace." or "I meditate peacefully."

You can make your own affirmation. The key is to use the present moment and believe what you are saying. Now, the matter of believing what you are saying may be difficult. After all, how can you believe something that you say that you know is just some form of wishful thinking and that the present reality is different? The key is to realize that what you say is possible, that it is all a matter of the mind. Therefore, if you adopt the right mindset, then it is no longer just wishful thinking but creates reality.

When it comes to making affirmations, there are a few points to consider: You must believe whatever it is that you affirm or say. You affirmation must be in the present tense. Last but not least, you must continue to do the affirmation until it works. Now, the third point should be qualified. Most people keep saying their affirmation on a regular basis, which means that they chant it many times. However, other people only mention their affirmation only once. Now, take note that both ways are correct and effective. The reason here is the presence and power of faith. Most beginners have to mention their affirmation many times before their mind can be influenced and take the proper mindset, while some advanced practitioners only need to mention it once, and they can already change their mindset. So, to avoid confusion, simply do what works for you.

It is not easy to avoid negative thoughts. They are simply very pushy and are good at getting one's attention. This is where self-mastery comes into play. Again, a good way to have self-mastery is also by persevering in your meditation practices.

The dark side of the mind usually reveals itself by bombarding you with negative thoughts. It will either make lots of negative thoughts to arise in your mind or simply use one or two negative thoughts that are extremely effective in distracting you. Either way, you will be faced with a big challenge of focusing on your mantra despite the great and very tempting distractions of the mind.

The mind is a very tricky thing. It is not uncommon for it to show you the strongest negative thought that you will find hard to ignore. The key to success when you encounter this is simply to stay true to your meditation. The more you allow yourself to be affected, the more you will lose focus. Unfortunately, some people at this point simply feel that they are not good enough to have any more progress and just drop their meditation practices thinking that they will never improve anymore. This is wrong. When the mind gets this tricky, you should have all the more reasons to stay strong. Although this may be a difficult stage to get pass through, you will usually experience a good reward in the form of bliss once you succeed it. The key is not to give up and continue on meditating. Instead of focusing on such negative thought or thoughts, simply be strong enough and focus on your meditation practice. The negative thought will not disappear right away, but if you do not pay any attention to it and just focus on your mantra, the said negative energy will disappear on its own — and you will be surprised just how much development you have achieved.

CHAPTER 4
Keys To Success

Here are some keys to success that will allow you to enjoy the best benefits of practicing meditation:

Continuous practice

Continuous practice is the key to meditation. As much as possible, try to meditate every day. Although you can practice different kinds of meditation, you should have one meditation technique that you should always practice. In meditation, the power of repetition is also important. So, be sure to meditate regularly. Among all the keys to success, this advice is the most important.

Develop your concentration

If you want to succeed in meditation, you need to have good concentration. Concentration simply refers to being able to focus on something without being distracted. Obviously, this is how all meditations should be — where you exist and experience the present moment and not get distracted. Most people care able to concentrate for a few seconds or minutes, but then notice that their mind starts to bombard itself with random thoughts after some time. If you are one of such people, then there is nothing for you to worry about because it is normal. Be kind and gentle to yourself and simply continue practicing. Regular practice of meditation naturally improves concentration. Another effective way to improve your concentration is by staring at an object. When you do, let nothing exist in your mind or consciousness but the object you are staring at. You can use any object that you want. It can be a pen, your mobile phone, or even your door frame. Do this for ten seconds, and then gradually increase the time. Stop when a thought that is not related to the object arises in the mind. Just give yourself maybe a few seconds to rest, and then start over. Be sure to do this regularly. You can also do this technique almost anytime and anywhere by simply closing your eyes and imagining the object.

Be one with the mantra

You need to have mastery of your mantra in order to be one with it. Once you have chosen a mantra that you want to use, keep saying it consciously, out loud or even just in your mind. Through continuous repetition, even your subconscious mind will get to know your mantra. In the beginning, when you meditate, you may have to put effort in saying your mantra. But, once you get used to your mantra, it will come naturally. In fact, you would not even have to chant it anymore. Instead, you will "hear" it being chanted on its own, and all that you have to do is close your eyes and meditate.

Another benefit if a mantra meditation is that you can use your mantra to trigger a pleasant state of mind even during normal or waking consciousness. For example, when you are feeling down or confused, simply chant your mantra, and you may notice feeling a glimpse of that bliss that you get when you meditate, which can help you get through a rough day. Of course, for this to work, you must have established a strong connection with your mantra.

Let go

When you meditate, you must learn to let go. Let go and free your soul. To let go also means to let go of any expectations and even beliefs. To simply be, without preferences or prejudices. Let go of what you want to happen. Instead, experience the present moment.

Live healthy

As mentioned in the first chapter of this book, the state of your energy body affects your physical body. It is also worth noting that the state of your physical body also affects your energy body. Therefore, it is important that you keep your physical body healthy. Learn to love healthy and follow a healthy diet.

Exercising is also good. In fact, doing physical exercises naturally strengthens your energy body. You do not have to be very fit to do this. You do not need to have six-pack abs. By simply improving your diet and living healthy, all your energy bodies, including your physical body, will also develop.

Introspection

Introspection or understanding one's self is important in meditation. The more you can understand yourself, the more you can control your thoughts. This is the time that you should judge yourself without any bias or prejudice. The important thing here is to be very honest with yourself. Although not necessary, you may find it helpful to use a journal to record your day-to-day meditation experiences, especially the challenges that you encounter. Do not worry; you do not have to be a professional writer to do this. Again, the important thing is for you to write as honest as you can. Keeping a journal will also allow you to think outside the box and see yourself from a different perspective. By doing so, you can get to think more clearly and understand yourself better.

When you do introspection, you have to identify your strengths and weaknesses. The objective is to increase your strengths and develop your weaknesses. This is why being brutally honest is important. Your journal should be a mirror of your soul. Unfortunately, many meditators do not accept their weaknesses. Just remember that the more honest you are in understanding yourself and in writing your journal, the better it will be for your development.

When engaged in introspection, think of the "mistakes" that you often encounter. Are there certain thoughts that keep repeating themselves in your mind? Try to find out why and what you can do to improve.

On a more spiritual note, the art of meditation is actually a deep sense of introspection. The practice of meditation will make you realize who you really are, as well as the oneness of everything else.

Learn to deal with distractions

It is worth noting that being distracted even during meditation is normal. Just as your body releases sweat or feels itchy, your mind releases so many thoughts. Just as sweating is a natural and important for the body, you should not see your thoughts as an enemy. Remember that before you can reach a state of no-mind, you must first be in a state where many thoughts are present. Be gentle and make peace with your thoughts by realizing that your thoughts are not an enemy. It is how you handle your thoughts that matter.

When distractions arise in the mind, you must remain calm and non-judgmental. Simply focus on your mantra or any point of focus of your meditation. You should not deal with distractions by being distracted. Rather, you conquer every distraction by simply doing the right thing.

Change

Do not be afraid to change. Regular practice of meditation can change a person for the better. As you continue to practice meditation, you may notice that you feel calmer and more focused. Remember that there is no development without a change, so learn to embrace positive changes in your life.

If the practice of meditation only makes you feel better but does not improve your personality, then you are not doing it right. All forms of meditation should make you a better person. Remember to always welcome positive changes in your life.

Continuous improvement

Always strive for continuous improvement. Even when you get good at meditating, do not stop doing introspection or looking for other ways to be better at meditating. A good way to get inspiration is to read and watch how Buddhist monks practice meditation. Also, pay attention to the discipline that they exercise. You can find many of these stories and videos online. Take note, however, that you should not view meditation as a form of competition. You do not compete against other meditators. Have you seen a saint saying or thinking that he is holier than another person? No, meditation does not work that way. Remember that meditation is a personal and spiritual pilgrimage.

Mindfulness

By intentionally focusing and fixing your attention on a fixed point, awareness increases and the mind becomes still. Also, you should not be judgmental of the moment. Instead, just accept everything as they truly are. Like a child, look at and feel everything as if it was the first time for you to experience anything. As you meditate, you may experience different states of awareness. In fact, even your emotions could change. In the midst of these changes, strive to keep an open mind. Just be conscious, and do not judge anything. Let everything unfold as they are; accept them as they are. Be mindful without intervening or being judgmental.

Although technically conscious and awake, most people are unconscious as to what happens from moment to moment. Unfortunately, for many, life has turned into a routine where every movement, breath, or second, is left unappreciated. Many get lost in their own thoughts that they fail to live and experience the present moment. As you practice meditation, you will be more aware and more present. What is more, you will be able to live this awareness and appreciation of life even after your actual practice of meditation. The more you practice mindfulness, the more you will be present in the moment of *Now*, which is the moment of being alive.

Keep it simple

Meditation is supposed to be easy and natural. Avoid doing meditations that have complex instructions; otherwise, you will end up analyzing and not meditating. Breathing and mantra meditations are simple and very effective. In fact, many monks spend years just meditating on their breath. It is also possible to achieve enlightenment even with the simplest meditation.

Detachment

Being detached is important in meditation. This means that you should be detached from your desires, ego, and even your thoughts and emotions. Detachment becomes easy when you realize that you are not the body nor the emotions nor the thoughts and that everyone and everything are connected. This is the oneness of spirituality. Of course, meditation is also the key to this realization.

Detachment also applies to your relationship with other people. You must be able to love without being too attached. Now, do not take this in a wrong way. You can and should love as much as you can. However, do not be selfish. Being so attached often leads to exercising undue control over the person you love. You should love a person as he or she is, and unconditionally. This is the secret to loving freely and without limitation. By detaching yourself from the one you love, you will be able to love him or her even more.

Understand your emotions

When you find that certain emotions are hard to ignore and prevents you from going deep into meditation, the best way to understand your emotions is to go directly to their roots. Unfortunately, many people are controlled by their emotions rather than the other way around. Most experiences in life give rise to various opportunities for emotions to take over one's life. Many think that emotions are what comprises their identity, and makes them who they are, which is wrong. Some people would think that it is okay to be angry or sad when someone has hurt them. Although logically normal, when you allow this, it creates a domino effect and makes you a slave to your own emotions, as well as the circumstances that give rise to such emotions.

It is worth noting that emotions are like thoughts that come and go. Just as you already know that you are not your thoughts, you should also realize that you are not your emotions. Now, you should consider this as good news, especially if your emotions are the ones causing you turmoil or suffering. This does not mean that emotions are bad. Like thoughts, emotions can always be used in your favor as long as you are able to control them.

The best way to control your emotions is to find out what has caused specific emotions to arise in your mind. Most negative emotions spring from anger, jealousy, envy, and others. What you should realize about these causes is that they cannot control you unless you allow them to take over your life. Most of the time, just by not acting or responding to such stimuli, you can avoid the harsh feelings that you experience with negative emotions. Also, emotions usually depend on one's experiences. By living a good and happy life, negative emotions can be minimized. In the face of challenges, where people act badly, the key to controlling your emotions is to exercise compassion. Remember that if someone does something wrong to you, it only reflects his own sadness. It should also be noted that according to Buddhist teachings, the mind is naturally pure.

Be kind

Being kind is a good way to easily increase one's vibration. Therefore, be kind at all times. The exercise of kindness is also a good way to increase your willpower, especially at times when being kind is simply not easy to do. For example, how can you be kind to someone who keeps on insulting you? But, be kind, anyway. If you are able to exercise kindness to a person who is mean, then you will be more easily able to express kindness to your loved ones.

When you meditate with kindness in your heart, you can easily tap a higher state of consciousness. Take note that you can never achieve enlightenment is you continue to harbor any form of hatred in your heart. Therefore, learn to exercise some compassion.

How to overcome the *self*

To reach higher states of consciousness, one needs to conquer the self. The self is full of desires and ego. Hence, to overcome the self, you need to overcome your desires by not clinging to them. When desire disappears, the ego also disappears. But desire is a tricky word. Does desire to improve in meditation and be enlightened considered bad? It does not mean that it is bad, but such desire will get in the way of your spiritual development. Remember that in meditation, nothing should exist but the point of your focus. If it is a mantra meditation, then only the mantra should exist. If you meditate on your breath, then only your breath should exist. If you follow the pathworking meditation in this book, then all your focus should be devoted to that, too. You must not desire anything else but simply "to be." Given the said example, say as you meditate, you also think of achieving enlightenment, your energy will be divided, and you cannot reach a stage where nothing exists but your mantra.

Compassion

If you read books on Buddhism, you will notice that the value of compassion is always given a special importance. However, this type of compassion is not something that is demanded or forced. Such compassion must be expressed with the heart. But, to do so, there must be realization. You simply cannot be truly compassionate when evil or anger broods in your heart. As usual, the key to developing compassion is to meditate regularly.

In Buddhism, compassion is a state of mind where you cherish other beings and sincerely wish for them to be freed from suffering. This, however, does not just mean a mere concern. For example, when your friend gets sick, you may wish for him to feel better, so you can play with him again. Now, this is not compassion. True compassion is about cherishing others, even without receiving any benefit from it. In today's world, the idea of compassion is a bit narrow and biased. In Buddhism, compassion takes a universal form, whether one experiences something bad or good. It is a sincere desire for another to achieve enlightenment and be completely free from suffering. Universal compassion can be attained through years of intense training.

Meditation is life

Meditation should not distance you from people, especially from your loved ones. Although many people these days meditate to relieve stress and feel better, the true effects of meditation are not really just for yourself, but also for others. Meditation should lead you to be kinder, express more love, and exercise compassion at all times. You must do so sincerely. The fact remains that even among those who meditate for years, only a few reach enlightenment in one lifetime. Therefore, although enlightenment may be your goal on why you meditate, never allow yourself to be obsessed with the idea of enlightenment. If you want to have less stress and live a happier life, then make peace with the people around you and show your love, even to your enemies. Meditation will give you the strength that you need to do so. All forms of meditation also develop the heart chakra, which will allow you to be more compassionate and exercise universal love.

CHAPTER 5
Answers to Common Questions

To further assist you in your spiritual journey, here are the answers to common questions about meditation:

Is it safe to practice meditation?

Generally, it is safe to practice meditation; however, there are meditation techniques that are not completely safe. Some meditation techniques require an intense form of discipline and could damage your chakras if not performed properly. The good news is that all the meditations in this book are completely safe.

How do I get started to meditate?

The only way to get started and truly learn meditation is simply by doing it. So, start meditating. Just choose a good time and place where you will not be distracted.

How long should I meditate?

You can meditate as much as you want. You can meditate for a few minutes, and you can also meditate for more than a day if you can. It is important that you focus on the quality of your meditation.

How do I know if I am doing it right?

You should understand that there is really no right and wrong way to meditate. Simply try whatever you want and see what works best for you. If you do not notice any progress in a few weeks, then try to make some adjustments. It is good to listen to your body and intuition.

How can I tell if I have achieved a high state of consciousness?

Each level has certain characteristics, which are described in the book. It is important to note that reaching a high state of consciousness should be seen as a mere result and not as an objective; otherwise, the very purpose of meditation would be lost. Regardless whether you are a beginner or not, your purpose for meditating should not be about reaching a high state of consciousness. Such kind of consciousness will naturally reveal itself as you progress in your spiritual journey.

Is it better to meditate in the morning?

The best time to meditate depends on the person. It varies. Many people find that meditating in the morning is easier because they feel more focused and not sleepy. However, others prefer meditating at night because it feels more peaceful and quiet. This depends on you and your lifestyle. If you want, you can meditate both in the morning and in the evening.

Should I use the same place for meditation?

Having one place where you meditate helps to focus the mind. By simply going to that place, it automatically signals the mind that it is time to meditate. However, this is not required. You can meditate anywhere you want. You might want to try different spots and see which one feels most comfortable for you.

Should I close my eyes when I meditate?

Again, this is a matter of personal preference. Many choose eto close those eyes to minimize distractions and to help them be more focused. Closing your eyes is also helpful when you engage in a pathworking meditation or where you need to imagine vivid sceneries. However, if you are comfortable meditating with your eyes open, then feel free to do that as well.

How long does it take to experience the benefits of meditation?

There is no hard and fast rule to this. You can already experience some benefits even if it is your first time to meditate. Other people usually experience the benefits after a few days. Meditating properly takes some practice. However, once you get the hang of it, you can experience the benefits of meditation every time you meditate, and even after meditation.

Will the practice of meditation give me psychic powers?

Yes. Meditation develops the chakras, which energizes your psychic senses. It is not uncommon for advanced meditators to share mystical and psychic experiences including being able to perform some magical feats. However, it should be noted that obtaining psychic powers should not be the purpose of your meditation. Also, such psychic powers only manifest when you reach a high level of spirituality and a natural effect of having highly developed chakras and a strong energy body.

Is meditation different from relaxation?

Yes. Relaxation is simply one of the common effects of meditation. Meditation can be considered a spiritual journey and is an active process where you remain aware and conscious of what you are doing. Meditation also offers more benefits than mere passive relaxation.

Is meditation against my religion?

Meditation is not barred by any religion. In fact, all the major religions in the world have their own meditation practices. Meditation is normal in spirituality. In fact, it can even be considered a need.

What is the best way to meditate?

There is no such thing as the better or best way to meditate. All forms of meditation lead to the same thing, which is enlightenment. Therefore, use the one that you think works best for you. If there were such thing as the best way, then that is simply to meditate as often as you can. Meditation is a life-long journey.

Any last tips?

Start meditating and persevere. I strongly recommend that you focus on learning the breathing or mantra meditation. You can also use other meditation techniques from time to time. Persevere and try to meditate every day. If you are a very busy person, you may find meditating at night as the best time to meditate. However, should you meditate at night, it is recommended that you do not meditate while lying down because it can easily trigger you to feel sleepy, especially when you are already tired after the day's work.

To learn more about meditation, it is good to read books on Buddhism and Hinduism. These spiritual paths hold the practice of meditation of great importance. You should also learn the teachings of Buddha.

To be a better meditator, cultivate a good and loving heart. Keep in mind that only those with a pure heart and mind can enter the highest states of consciousness. To have a good heart and mind, learn from your loved ones and from your enemies. Your loved ones will encourage you to love, while your enemies will teach you many important values.

Do not be too hard on yourself. The practice of meditation is not supposed to be hard. It must come naturally, without any tension or pressure.

If you can, try to learn to meditate in the evening just before going to sleep, so that you will not have to worry about the time. When meditating, it is easy to lose track of time, especially when you go deep into the meditation.

If you are interested in mantra meditation, then learn to be one with your mantra. Chant your mantra even when not meditating. Let it seep into your soul that you can hear it echo on its own. When you reach this kind of connection with your mantra, you only need to close your eyes to "hear" it. This means that you no longer have to physically chant it over and over again, which will allow you to focus on it even more. Also, avoid changing your mantra. When you change your mantra, you will have to work on building a connection with it over again.

It is also helpful to find befriend people who are also interested in meditation. This will help boost your interest, and can also be a good way to learn more about meditation. Also, practicing meditation is a group makes it easier to reach a higher state of consciousness. This is because of the effect of the group consciousness that is formed. Just be sure that the people that you meditate with are truly passionate and interested in meditation.

You should also realize that meditation is only a part of spirituality and that spirituality does not refer to meditation alone. Here is the secret: Spirituality is life. Live a good life, surround yourself with people who love you and love them without end, and you will have the best spirituality you can ever ask for.

CONCLUSION

Thank you for making it through to the end of this book. I hope it was informative and able to provide you with all of the tools you need to achieve your goals, whatever they may be.

The next step is to start trying some of these techniques in your life and find out what works best for you.

Finally, if you found this book useful in any way, a review on Amazon is always appreciated! -Sarah Rowland

DESCRIPTION

Meditation for Beginners: Ultimate Guide to Relieve Stress, Depression, and Anxiety is your one-stop guide that will teach you everything that you need to know about meditation.

Learn:

- What meditation is
- The basics of meditation
- Different meditation techniques
- To use meditation to relieve stress, anxiety, and depression
- The different states of consciousness
- Common pitfalls
- Keys to success

And so much more!

This book is the handy manual that will change your life and free yourself from negative energies. *NOW* is the time to make a change and live a happier life.

www.ingramcontent.com/pod-product-compliance
Lightning Source LLC
Chambersburg PA
CBHW071506070526
44578CB00001B/460